KALEIDATONAL HEARING

Melodic and Harmonic Dictation in Tonal Music

by

MICHAEL G. CUNNINGHAM

Technical book set-up by

ADAM BOLL

STUDENT MANUAL

AuthorHouse™
1663 Liberty Drive, Suite 200
Bloomington, IN 47403
www.authorhouse.com
Phone: 1-800-839-8640

First published by AuthorHouse 1/14/2009

ISBN: 978-1-4389-4251-3 (sc)

Printed in the United States of America
Bloomington, Indiana

This book is printed on acid-free paper.

Table of Contents

Clapping Rhythms

Clap the rhythm while saying the beats. Perform each exercise three times without pause.

E.T.

Test No. 1

Name: _____

M *lm* / d / A

1.

3. Only M3, P5, P8

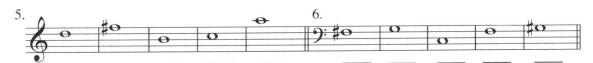

7. 8. 9.

10. 11.

Only M & m

Ⓧ

a. b. c.

d. e.

- 3 -

E.T.

Test No. 2

Name: _____

E.T.   # Test No. 3   Name: _____

Test No. 4

Name: _____

M / m / d / A

1. ⑤

2. ④

3. Add M7, M2

4.

5.

6.

7. Add and

8.

9.

10.

X ④

1 2 3 4 5 6 7 8   8 7 6 5 4 3 2 1

a.

b.

c.

d.

Test No. 5

Name: _____

Test No. 6

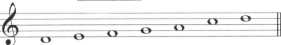 

  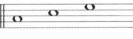

  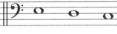

 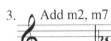

Major - minor Scales I

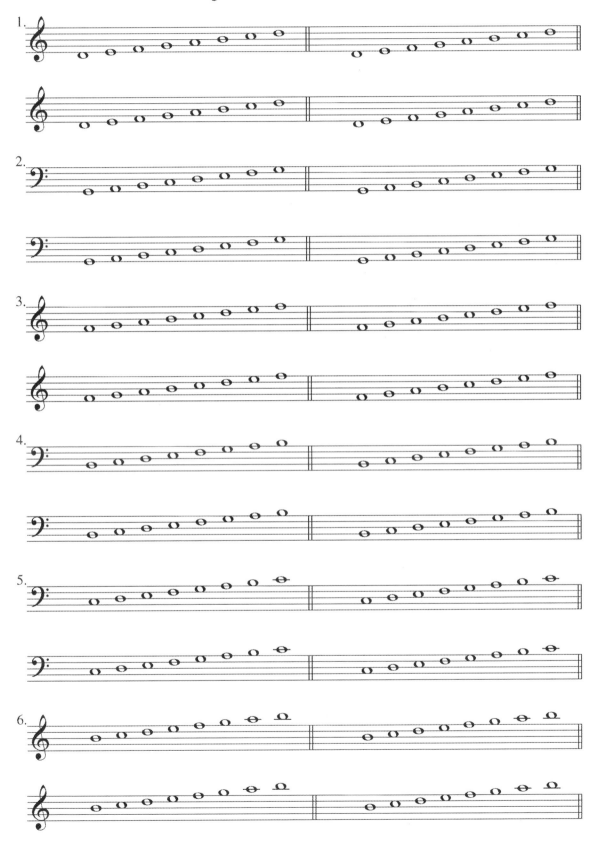

Major - minor Scales II

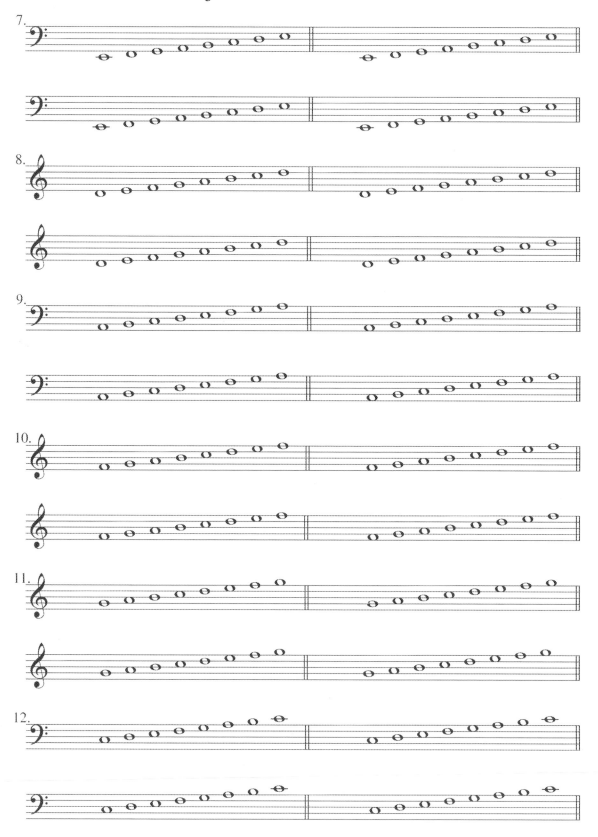

Where's the Tonic I

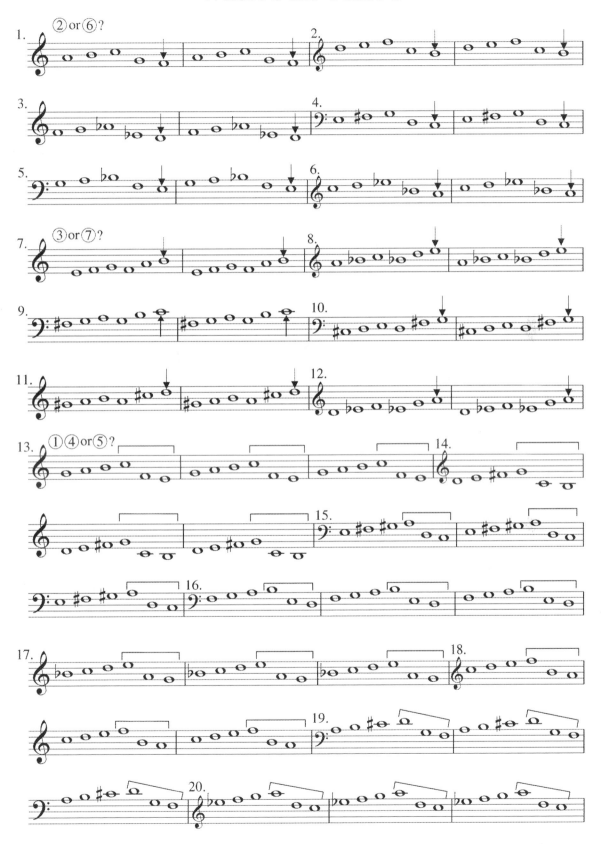

Melodic Dictation

1. Little Bo Peep (1685) Elizabeth (Mother) Goose
2. Anchors Aweigh (1906) Melody: Charles Zimmerman
3. Westminster Chimes (1793) William Crotch
4. Caissons Go Rolling Along (1918) Edward L. Gruber
5. Goodnight Ladies (1853) Centonized
6. Hail, Hail, The Gang's All Here (1917) Theodore Morse
7. My Bonnie Lies Over the Ocean (1881) Scottish: Unknown
8. For He's a Jolly-Good Fellow (1783) Centonized

Melodic Dictation

9. When the Saints Go Marching In (1896)   Melody: James M. Black

10. Little Brown Jug (1869)   Joseph E. Winner

11. Auld Lang Syne (1687)   Unknown (Later poetry by Robert Burns)

12. Mary Had a Little Lamb (1867)   Sara Hale

13. The Halls of Montezuma (1868)   Melody: Jules Offenbach

14. Reveille (1831)   Unknown (French)

15. Aura Lee (1861)   George R. Roulton

16. Hickory Dickory Dock (c. 1750)   Elizabeth F. Goose

17. This Old Man (?)   Unknown

18. National Emblem (1906)   E. E. Bagley

Melodic Dictation

19. Battle Hymn of the Republic (1861)   Unknown

20. Sailor's Hornpipe (1796)   Unknown

21. Camptown Races (1850)   Stephen Foster

22. I Dream of Jeanie (1845)   Stephen Foster

23. My Old Kentucky Home, Goodnight (1853)   Stephen Foster

24. Oh Susanna (1848)   Stephen Foster

25. Old Folks at Home (1851)   Stephen Foster

26. Some Folks (1855)   Stephen Foster

Melodic Dictation

Triads

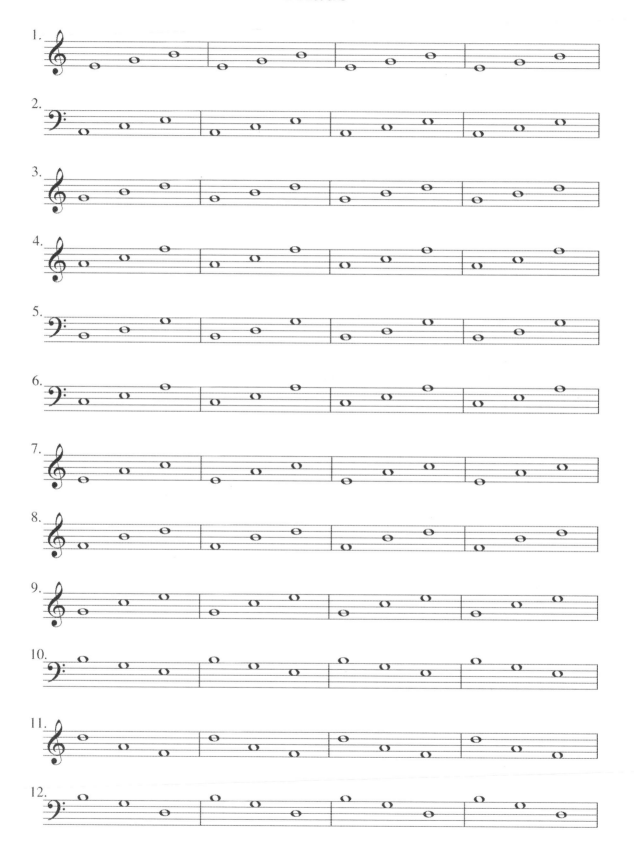

Melodic Dictation

27. Semper Fidelis (1888)   J.P. Sousa

28. The Thunderer (1889)   J.P. Sousa

29. Washington Post (1889)   J.P. Sousa

30. High School Cadets (1890)   J.P. Sousa

31. Manhattan Beach (1893)   J.P. Sousa

32. Liberty Bell (1893)   J.P. Sousa

Triads

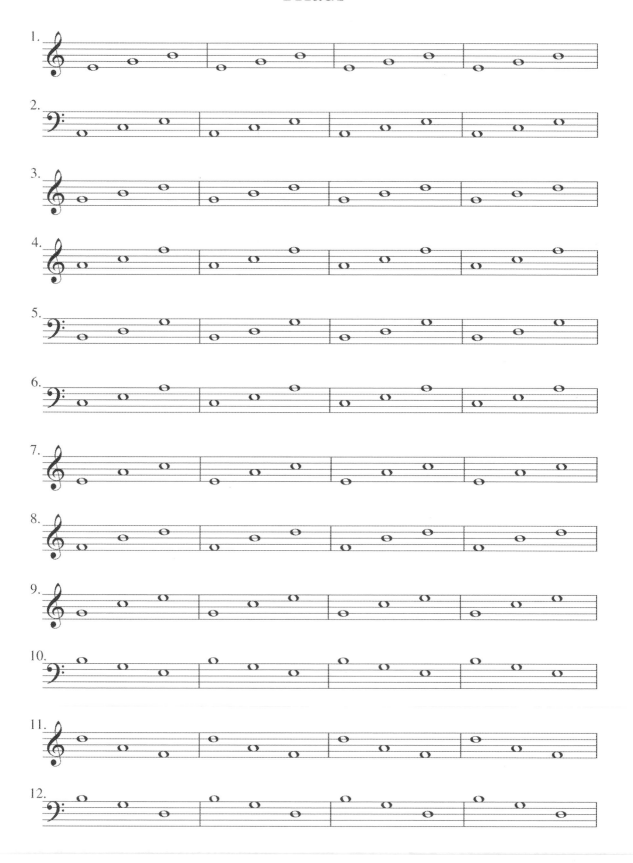

Triads

Five-Step Exercise

Basic Harmonic Units

Structural Progressions

Teacher Directed Drills and Games

1. OCTAVE LEAPS: Since many students miss octave leaps during melodic dictation, the following should be individually sung in class.

2. RAMEAU BOXES: Respond as follows, one at a time, indicating what you hear in the soprano. The later exercise focuses on the bass notes. Just put boxes, letters and numbers.

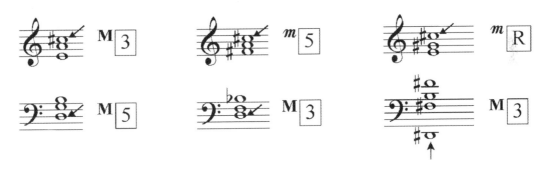

3. SINGING CHORDS: In a determined scale that suits your voice, sing the primary triads as follows:

> Major: 1-3-5, 4-6-1, 5-7-2, 1-3-5. Or do-mi-sol, fa-la-do, sol-ti-re, do-mi-sol.
> In minor: 1-3-5, etc. or la-do-mi, etc.

4. POINTING AT NOTES ON THE BOARD: If called upon, go to the board and respond as directed, remembering that all the other class members will be experiencing the exercise through you. All will be simultaneously engaged in positive "tonality-thinking."

PART II
SECOND SEMESTER EXERCISES

Melodic Dictation of Folk and Americana Melodies

a b   Barbara Allen   (1666)   Unknown

a b c d   Thanksgiving Prayer-We Gather Together(1630)   Adrian Valerie?

a a b a (Ballad)   The Girl I Left Behind   (1650)   Unknown

a a' a' b   The Riddle (I Gave My Love a Cherry)   (1785)   Unknown

* "Folk" melodies were created by unknown individuals.

- 30 -

a a' a b

Oh Dear, What Can the Matter Be? (1778)

Unknown

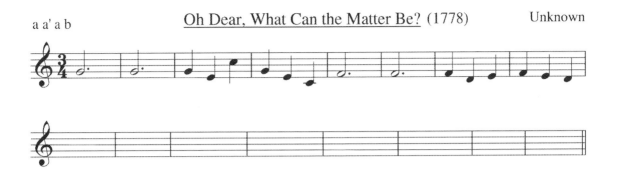

a b

Billy Boy   (1824)

Unknown

a a b a (Ballad)

The Blue Bell of Scotland (1815)

Unknown

a b

On Top of Old Smoky (1841)

Unknown

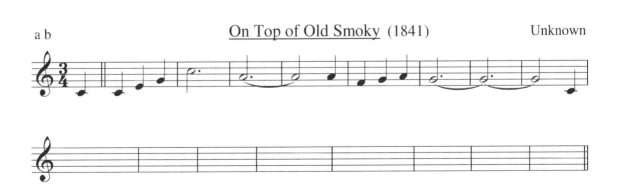

a a b a (Ballad)   <u>All Through the Night</u>   (1825)   Unknown

a b c a   <u>Charlie is My Darling</u>   (1830)   Unknown

a a' a b   <u>Skip to My Lou</u>   (1832)   Unknown

aaba (Ballad)

Flow Gently Sweet Afton
(1838)

Unknown
1789 Poem: Robert Burns

(C Major - the "bridge")

(F Major)

aaba (Ballad)

Long, Long, Ago   (1843)

Thomas Bayley

a a¹a²a³

Blue-Tail Fly   (1848)

Daniel D. Emmett

Blow the Man Down (1849)

Unknown

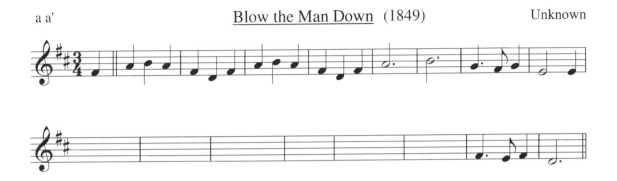

a b c a

Sweet Betsy From Pike (1851)

Unknown

a b

Pop Goes the Weasel (1853)

Charles Twigg (?)

a b Loch Lomond (1881 or 1746?) Scottish: Unknown

a a b a (Ballad) The Minstrel Boy (1813) Unknown

a a b a (Ballad) The Ash Grove (Date ?) Welsh: Unknown

Sequence- - - - - - - - - - - - - - - -｜ Sequence - - - - - - - - - - - - - - - - -｜

a a b a (Ballad) <u>Believe Me, If All Those Endearing Young Charms</u> Irish: Unknown
(1810)

a a b a (Ballad) <u>In the Gloaming</u> (1877) Annie F. Harrison

a a b a (Ballad) <u>The Loreley</u> (Date ?) Friederich Silcher

A♭ Major

D♭ Major

- 38 -

- 39 -

a b a c (Bifid) <u>She'll Be Comin' 'Round the Mountain</u> (1899) American
Black: Unknown

a b a c (Bifid) <u>Oh, Dem Golden Slippers</u> (1879) James A. Bland

a a' b c <u>I've Been Working on the Railroad</u> (Part 1, 1881) Unknown
(The Levee Song)

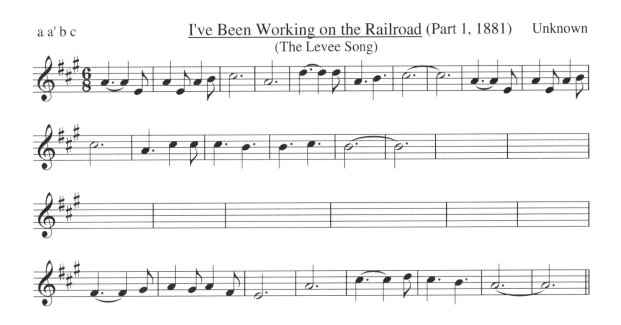

a a b b
My Bonnie Lies Over the Ocean (1875)   Scottish: Unknown

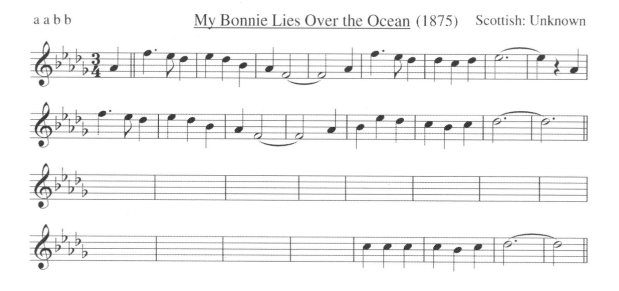

a b a b (Bifid)
Clementine (1884)   Percy Montrose

a b a c (Bifid)
Love's Old Sweet Song (1887)   James Lyman Molloy

a b a c (Bifid)   **Daisy Bell** (1892)   Henry Dacre

a b c b   **The Sidewalks of New York** (1894)   Charles Lawler

a a¹b a² (Ballad)   **Meet Me in Saint Louis** (1904)   Frederick Allen Mills

a b c b   In the Good Old Summertime (1902)   Shields and Evans

a b a c (Bifid)   In My Merry Oldsmobile (1905)   Gus Edwards

Modes I

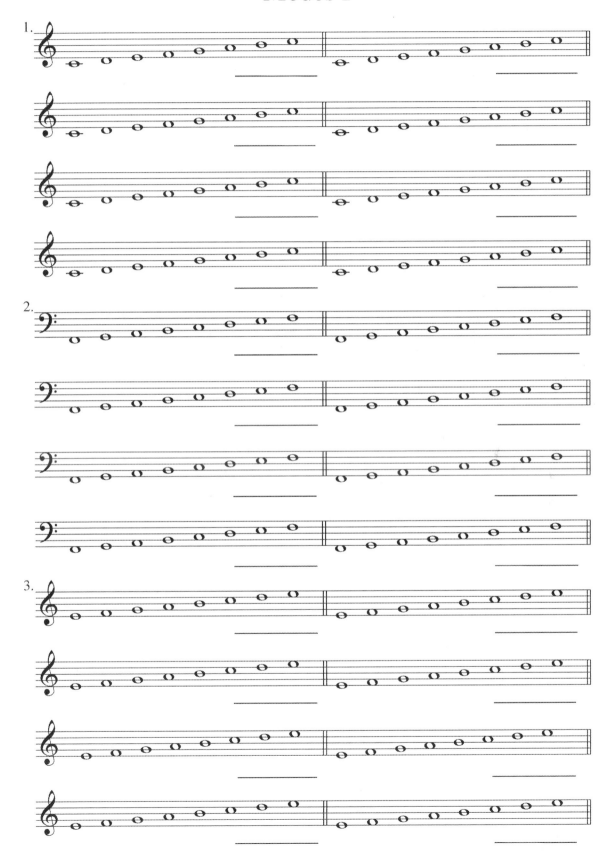

Modes II

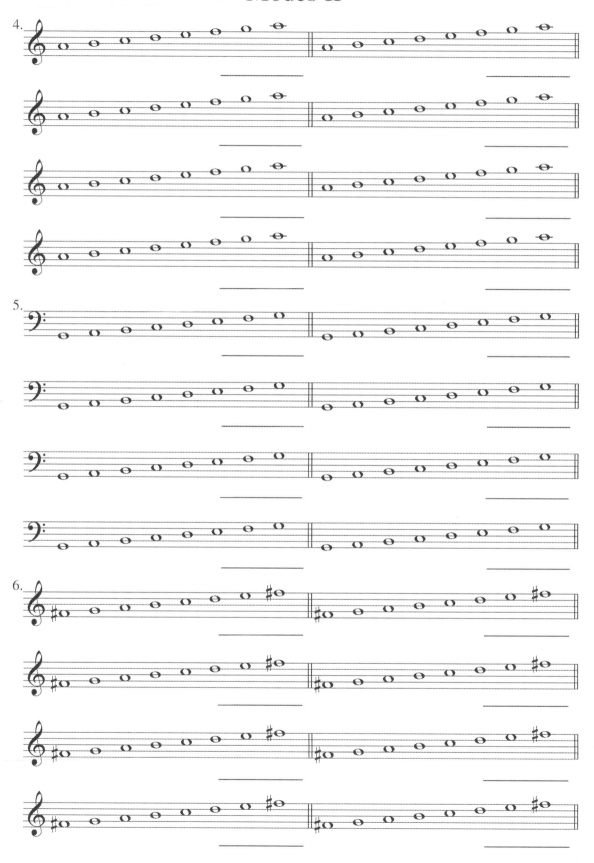

Modes III

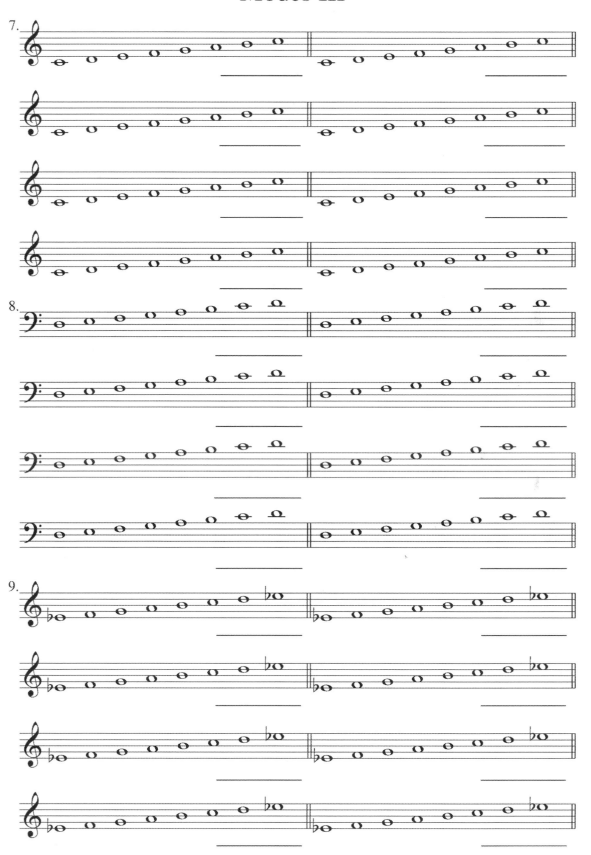

Modes IV

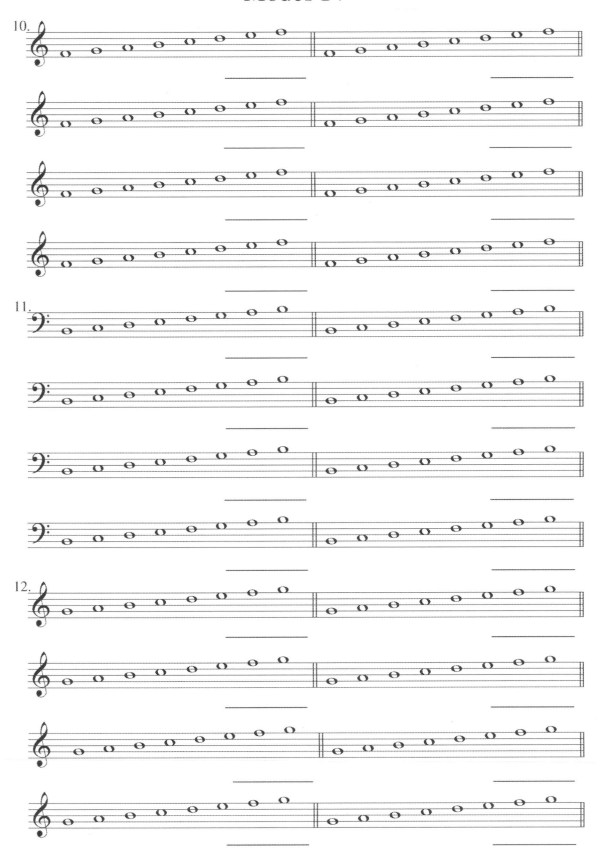

Ear Training Drill #1

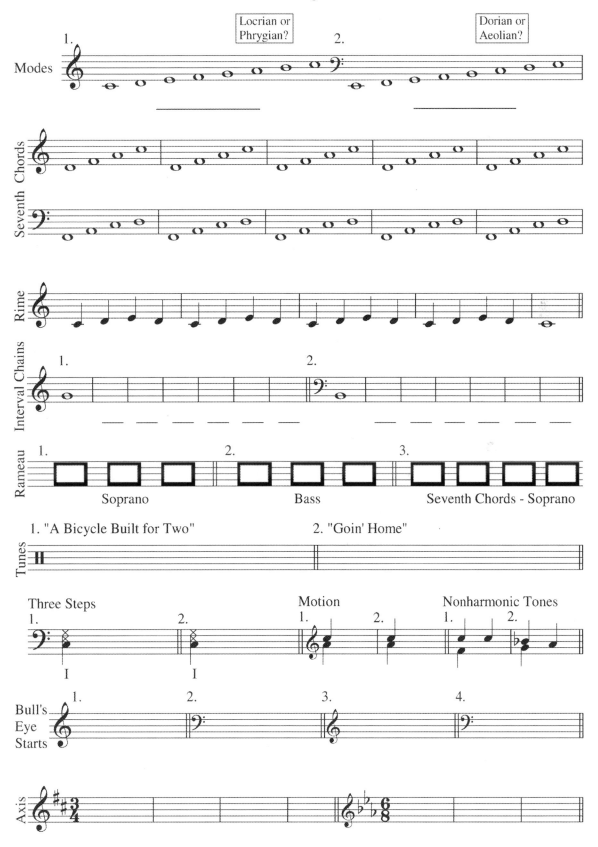

Ear Training Drill #2

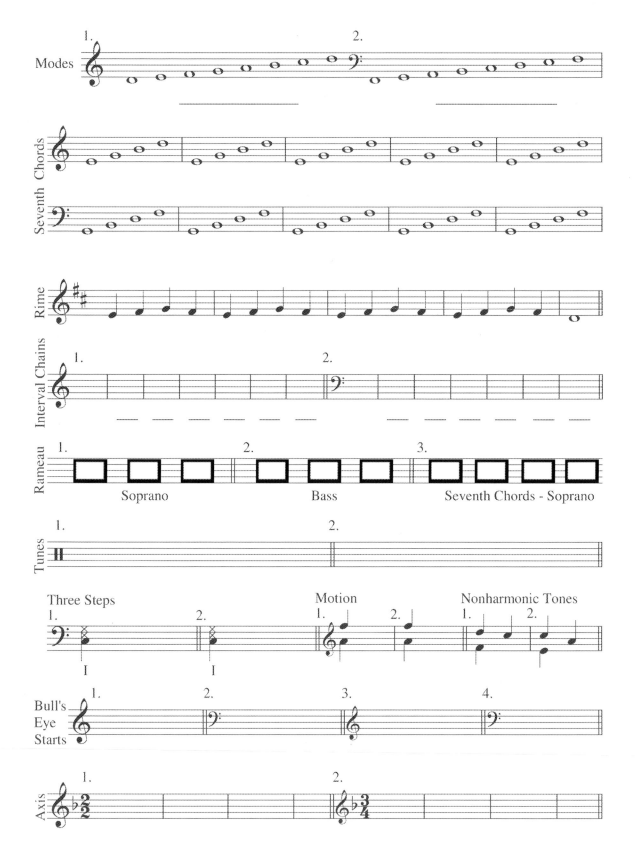

Ear Training Drill #3

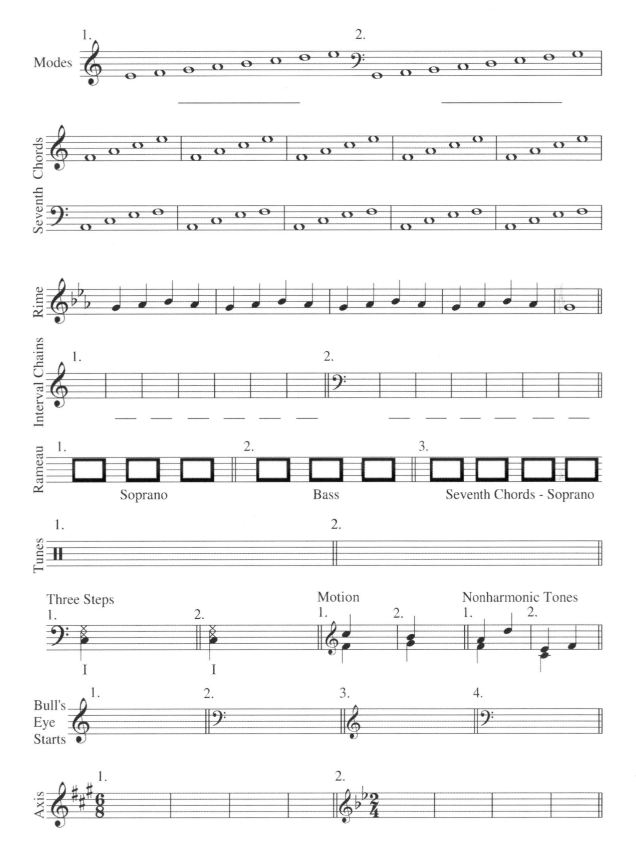

Ear Training Drill #4

Ear Training Drill #5

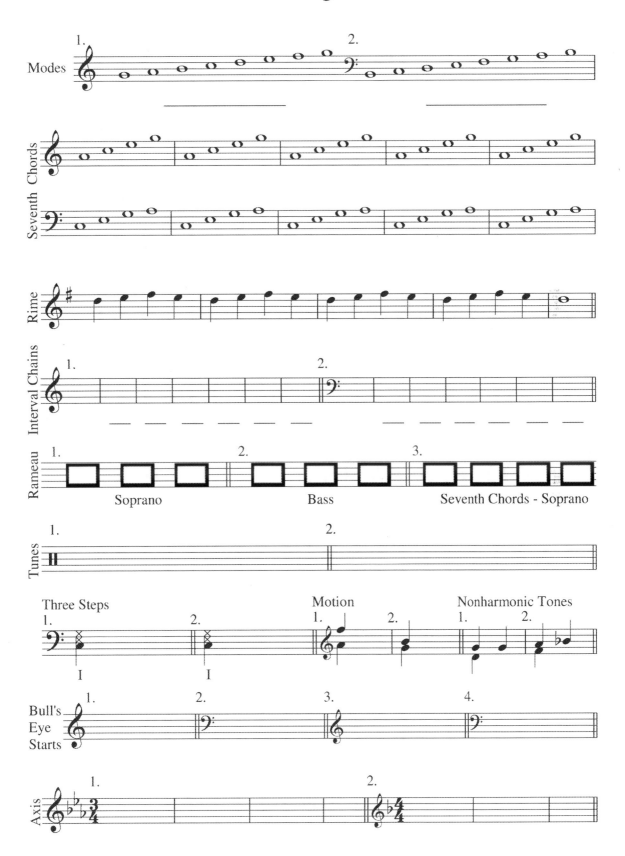

Ear Training Drill #6

Ear Training Drill #7

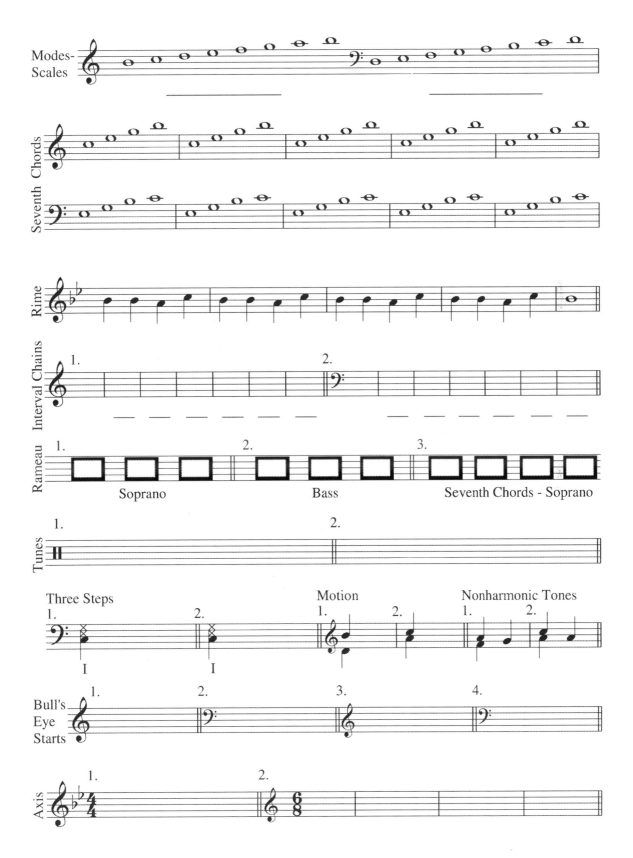

More Interval Chains

1.

2.

3.

4.

5.

6.

7.

8.

9.

10.

11.

12.

13.

14.

15.

16.

17.

18.

19.

20.

21.

22.

23.

24.

More $\frac{6}{8}$ Meter Rhythmic/Tonic/Dominant Axis Dictation

More Bull's Eye Starts

1 2 3 4

5 6 7 8

9 10 11 12

13 14 15 16

17 18 19 20

21 22 23 24

25 26 27 28

29 30 31 32

33 34 35 36

37 38 39 40

41 42 43 44

45 46 47 48

More Seventh Chords I

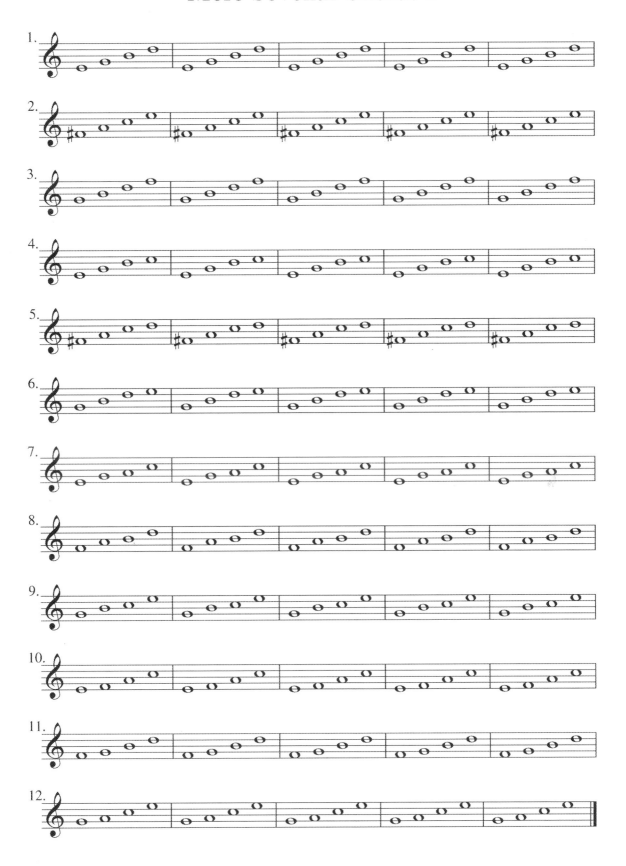

Seventh Chords II

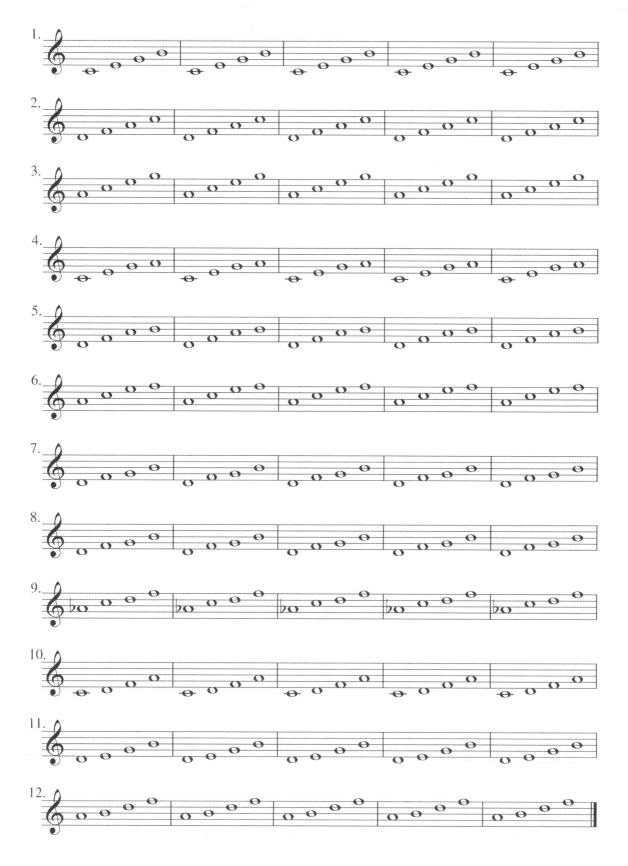

Four Kinds of Motion

More Nonharmonic Tones

All exercises are in $\frac{4}{4}$

Harmonic Similarities I

Harmonic Similarities II

V_5^6 or vii^{d7}

7. a. b. c.

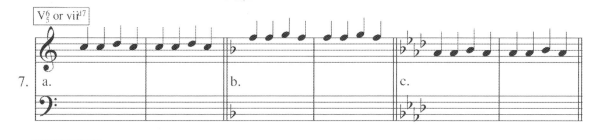

vii^{d7} or vii^{ø7}

8. a. b. c.

ii^7 or $V_{/V}^7$

9. a. b. c.

$V_5^6/_V$ or vii$^{d7}/_V$

10. a. b. c.

IV or N^6

11. a. b. c.

vii$^{d7}/_V$ or Ger^6

12. a. b. c.

Key Stability I

Key Stability II

Special Etudes

Mozart Melodies I

Mozart Melodies II

Mozart Melodies III

Mozart Melodies IV

Mozart Melodies V

Put the changed chord in the blank measure, along with the chord symbol.

Harmonic Rime

Non-Dominant Seventh Chords

Secondary Dominants I

Secondary Dominants II

Phrygian Cadences   (III is V of Relative minor)

Brief Modulations to Relative Major (Pivot Chords)

Other Modulations

Chromatic Chords I
Put changed chords in the blank measure along with the two surrounding chords.

Chromatic Chords II

Harmonic Rime

Seventh Chords

1.) M M

2.) M m

3.) m m

4.) d m⌀

5.) M M

6.) M m

7.) m m

8.) d m⌀

9.) M M

10.) M m

11.) m m

12.) d m⌀